Parables of a Rancher's Life

Frank W. Jones III

Parables of a Rancher's Life
Copyright © 2014 Frank W. Jones III
http://www.angelcanyonpublishing.com/author-frank-w-jones/

ISBN-13: 978-1497390300
ISBN-10: 1497390303

Cover design by J.P. Ruiz
PO Box 924, Utopia, TX 78884
johnnypruiz@authorjpruiz.com

All rights reserved. No part of this publication may be reproduced, stored in retrievable system, or transmitted in any form or by any means – electronic, mechanical, photocopying, recording, or otherwise – without the prior written permission of the publisher or the author. The only exception is brief quotations in printed reviews or the use of this material in Bible Studies.

Angel Canyon Publishing House
PO Box 924, Utopia, Texas 78884
www.angelcanyonpublishing.com
johnnypruiz@authorjpruiz.com

DEDICATION

    I would like to dedicate this book of parables to my beautiful and gracious wife, Darlene, who so faithfully interpreted my writings for the newsletters of the United Methodist Church and Living Waters Church in Utopia. I am so thankful for the Holy Spirit showing me the stories that were part of my life experiences and the scriptural lessons that were revealed to me. In writing these, my prayer is that the Holy Spirit will speak to anyone who would be drawn to read them.

                                          God Bless You,

                                          Frankie Jones III

ACKNOWLEDGEMENTS

    I want to thank my wife for taking so much time in typing all these stories for me no matter what they were written on. Some on paper towels , some on yellow pads, some in my cattle record books, and maybe some on feed sacks covered in grease. I appreciate her so much for helping me out , we are one. I would also want to thank Johnny Ruiz for his help in putting these stories in book form for me. I couldn't have done it without you Brother, thanks.

God bless you,
Frank W. Jones III

Foreword

I thank God for the day He chose to place Frankie Jones in my life. Frankie has walked through my good and bad times and remains my friend and brother in Christ. Frankie is not one who will only stand behind you, but he will grab your hand and pull you through it. I know Jesus is always there for me and will never forsake me, but I must say that I feel so loved that Jesus cares so much about me to give me a friend such as Frankie. Frankie and his family are part of my family and we are blessed beyond belief because of it.

This book is a must have, and will make a wonderful gift to anyone you know (and those you don't know). The stories are simple but are so rich in Christian principal. This book is what everyone needs to have on their desk at work or coffee table at home. These stories do not just teach lessons but they inspire, and inspiration is what this world hungers for in this day and age. God loves you so much that He gave His one and only Son Jesus to come to earth and die for your sins so that you may spend eternity with Him (John 3:16). Jesus loves you so much that he places Godly men such as Frankie on this earth to lead and inspire us as an example through his stories and the manner in which he lives his life.

This is not a book that is meant to look good sitting in your library collection. I believe, just as Jesus taught by using parables, the parables contained in this book are here to be read over and over again. They will always be fresh and speak new revelations into your life. They will help you grow in your Christian walk with practical applications. Always keep a copy handy to give away. I know Frankie is a Holy Spirit Filled Christian and I have no doubt that this book was inspired by the Holy Spirit.

"For I know the plans I have for you," declares the LORD, *"plans to prosper you and not to harm you, plans to give you hope and a future. Then you will call on me and come and pray to me, and I will listen to you. You will seek me and find me when you seek me with all your heart."* ---Jer. 29: 11-13

Blessings,

Johnny P. Ruiz

Published Author

(The Father's Love, and The Sam Series of Christian children's books)

www.authorjpruiz.com

Introduction

The following stories were given to Brother Frankie from the Holy Spirit during a season in his life for such a time as this. It is so amazing how Jesus works through the power of the Holy Spirit. He not only provides guidance but emotional support and comforting. During the time of Jesus on the earth he taught using parables, not as an encoded message, but a message that was appropriate for the time. According to Dictionary.com, the definition of a Parable is, "a short allegorical story designed to illustrate or teach some truth, religious principle, or moral lesson; a statement or comment that conveys a meaning indirectly by the use of comparison, analogy, or the like." You see Jesus knew that in order for the people to better understand His message he would need to use parables. In the same way the stories in this book convey a message that is true to our time and provide a greater understanding of the message of Jesus Christ for our lives today.

Brother Frankie is such an inspirational messenger and prophetic soldier of the Kingdom of Heaven. The stories contained in this book provide special meaning to the work of Jesus Christ in the world today as it applies to us in the simplest of situations. Jesus cares about the smallest things just as much as the enormous problems that try to engulf our lives. The stories Brother Frankie writes give direction and provide a clear vision of the lessons God gives us in everything we experience.

As it states in 1 Corinthians 13, without love we have nothing and love is certainly the reason the Holy Spirit provides us with such great direction as He has through the stories contained in this book. The message is clear and entertaining, but the meaning will bring you through the toughest of times through the power of the Gospel of Jesus Christ. Enjoy your reading and don't keep it to yourself.

Contents

FOREWORD vi

INTRODUCTION viii

A CRIPPLED TURKEY 2

A RED HORSE MINNOW 8

A WORD FROM GOD 11

A WORD FROM GOD (II) 12

ARE YOU WEARING ASBESTOS? 18

DEAR JESUS 25

DO YOU HAVE A CRACK IN YOUR CAULK? 27

FEED MY SHEEP 29

FOR MEN ONLY 32

GATHERING ANGORA GOATS 36

GOING IN THE SURVIVAL CAVE 40

GOING ON A DEER SURVEY 44

GOING SHRIMPING 48

GOING UP IN THE HEMISPHERE TOWER 51

HARVESTING DAVID'S WHEAT 54

HOW TO SPROUT A MOUNTAIN LAUREL SEED 57

HUNTIN' IN COLORADO 61

KILLING BRUSH 64

LATE WINTER BURN 67

LEARNING TO SWIM 70

LEE SELLERS MADE A DIFFERENCE 73

LOOKING FROM THE MOUNTAIN TOP	76
LOOKING THROUGH THE LENS OF A CAMERA	80
MANAGING BEAR CREEK RANCH	82
"A FATHER & SON"	82
MUTT AND JEFF	85
MY COWS KNOW MY VOICE	87
MY LINKAGE WAS FROZEN UP	90
MY TURBO BLEW OFF	93
OLD SUNNY	96
OUR OLD RANCH TRUCK	100
PLANTING KLEIN GRASS SEED	103
AUGUST 2002	103
PRUNING FRUIT TREES	106
SINGEING DOVES	109
SOWING WILD OATS	112
TEJIN AND RUSTY,	114
GETTING CUT IN LIFE'S BATTLES	114
WHAT'S COOKING IN THE KITCHEN?	120
WHO OR WHAT IS CONTROLLING YOUR LIFE?	123
WHOSE VOICE DO YOU LISTEN TO?	126
WORKING CLAY WITH MAMA GLADYS	129

Parables of a Rancher's Life   Frank W. Jones III

A Crippled Turkey

Last year while I was filling feeders for deer and turkey season, I noticed a turkey that had been crippled by a hunter or some other means. This turkey was hurt and would not get into the flock for fear that he might get injured again. He would stay on the perimeters, but would never get to feed. He would just watch and wait hoping to get some leftovers.

As the year went on the crippled bird just got farther and farther away until I stopped seeing the bird at all with the flock. I saw the turkey a few times by himself trying to feed on some feed that the squirrels would knock out, however food wasn't enough; he needed the fellowship and strength of the flock. Finally the turkey disappeared and one day I found a pile of feathers. I guess a predator had caught him and killed him.

We must be real careful not to let ourselves be hurt to the point where we get out of fellowship with the body of Christ. When we do we miss the blessing of the corporate anointing that comes with the body of Christ, being in one accord, like praise, worship, prayer, and receiving and applying the spoken word of God. That is where we find signs and wonders, miracles, deliverance, redemption, and revelation.

So when we get separated out of or separate ourselves out of the corporate body of Christ we are more subject to the predators of life. Predators prey on weak things that are more easily caught so you might be destroyed or you might join the group of predators and become a predator yourself. So what will we do? We will circle the wagons when trouble comes our way and join in the body of Christ for help and protection and we will join in the body of Christ also for praise, worship, and ministry.

Your brother in Christ Jesus,

Frankie Jones

Hebrews 10:25…Let us not give up meeting together, as some are in the habit of doing, but let us encourage one another and all the more as you see the day approaching.

Acts 42-43…They devoted themselves to the apostle's teaching and to the fellowship, to the breaking of bread and to prayer. Everyone was filled with awe, and many wonders and miraculous signs were done by the apostles.

1 Peter 5:8…Be self-controlled and alert. Your enemy, the devil, prowls around like a roaring lion looking for someone to devour.

6/15/2003

A Million Dollar Story

Suppose you received a letter giving you a map and directions to find and receive $1,000,000.00. All you have to do is to find this big, white house that has specific directions how to get there. Then your letter says that the money is inside, just seek it and you will find it. So you begin to look in all the rooms of the house. You look in the cabinets, closets, icebox, freezer, under the table, and everywhere you can think of in your mind. Finally you come upon a room with a glass door and a person is sitting behind the door. Out of respect, you knock without any hesitation because you know that there is a $1,000,000.00 just waiting for you on the other side. So you knock and ask if you can come in and the person says sure, come in and receive the treasure you have been called to find.

It seems so hard sometimes to find Jesus when it is really so easy. We keep looking for Him in the wrong places. We keep looking for Him in the things of the world that make us feel happy, when all the time He is behind the glass door just waiting and calling out to us to just look my way and you can see that I am here. Just open the glass door and ask to come in and He will abide with you and you with Him. Then you will begin to receive treasures He has in store for you. Then you will be able to find happiness in all things not just in a million dollars.

Matthew 6:33 says, "*Seek first his kingdom and his righteousness, and all these things will be given to you as well.*"

Matthew 7:7&8 says, "*Ask and it will be given to you; seek and you will find; knock and the door will be opened to you. For everyone who asks receives; he who seeks finds; and to him who knocks, the door will be opened.*"

By: Frank Jones III

A Red Horse Minnow

Have you ever been fishing with a red horse minnow? It's a real blast and usually very successful because they are lively and have bright red fins and tails. As kids we, meaning usually any combination of Kent, Murray, Sid Jr., Bob, and I would go to our favorite spots on the river and Mill Creek to seine for minnows, always trying to catch at least some red horse minnows.

One day while fishing in the old Schimmelfinney hole, which is between Taylor Crossing and Clarence LeBouf's house, my fishing buddies and I were on a mission to catch fish with a fresh batch of red horse minnows and some schinners. I knew this hole where the over-hanging brush from the other side offered good cover for those old moss back bass. The water was so clear you had to be really cautious not to let the fish see you because they would know that something was going on. I selected a perfect red horse minnow and, with my Mitchell 300 reel, cast it out in front of the brush cover. The minnow went to work darting and wiggling sending out the perfect lure to the old moss back bass. Sure enough he came out! My heart was pumping with excitement. As he eased out and came close, the minnow disappeared into his mouth. I jerked the rod and to my disappointment the bass spit out the bait and I never saw that old moss back bass again.

God throws out bait to us all the time. He is always trying to catch us to put His spirit into us so we will work the plan He has for us in our lives. Unlike me where I jerked the line too soon, He will never jerk the bait, the gifts, out of us. However, I'm afraid that many times we spit out the bait, the gifts, rather than giving in to Him and allowing ourselves to be hooked by God. Many times, I'm afraid, we won't even try to take the bait and just run away before we even taste it. If the bass had swallowed the bait his purpose would have been to bring me pleasure in the fishing experience and the meal.

If we take the bait, the gifts of the Holy Spirit, we will be empowered to do God's work in our lives even into eternity. Take the bait and swallow it.

> Your brother in Christ,
>
> Frankie Jones III

John 5:24... "Most assuredly, I say to you, he who hears My word and believes in Him who sent Me has everlasting life, and shall not come into judgment, but has passed from death into life."

James 1:17... Every good gift and every perfect gift is from above, and comes down from the Father of lights, with whom there is no variation or shadow of turning.

Revelation 3:20... "Behold, I stand at the door and knock. If anyone hears My voice and opens the door, I will come in to him and dine with him, and he with Me."

06/20/00

A Word from God

Why do you worship Me in programs and ritual? For I am spirit so you must worship Me in spirit and in truth. For when you worship Me in spirit I will lift you up. For the physical can only manifest the physical, but the spirit manifests the spirit. The spirit can manifest the physical for I have created the heavens and the earth from the spirit. Thus says the Lord.

06/10/02

A Word from God (II)

Make way a path for I am going to move rapidly across the nations of the earth. I will pour out my spirit on my people. Prepare your hearts because you will endure many tests.

6/10/2001

A Word from the Lord (III)

Many things have been happening to people lately and being distressed and burdened about it, I asked the Lord in prayer, "What is all this about?" This is the word I believe that I received.

These things are happening because we are entering into a time of enlightenment for there are many that are in a place of sheol. I asked what that was and He said, "A place of holding where they are not going forward or backward but they will be enlightened and they will know that I am the Lord thy God."

A Worn Out Planter

About thirty years ago in the 1970s, our seed drill wore out and I found a good used one in Goliad. This seed drill was just what we needed, so I purchased it for the ranch. It not only had a grain drill, but, also, a grass seeder for very small grass seeds.

This was a timely purchase because we were embarking in a new direction of planting Klein grass in most of our fields. This seed drill could plant the grass seed very shallow and precisely for optimum germination and sprouting. It also planted oats, wheat, and grazers for many years successfully.

After many years, the scraper wore out; the disks wore out; the tension springs and the connecting points wore out. I began to start getting a bad stand with many weeds and was limited to dry planting in only very clean soil.

Dad and I decided to purchase a new seed drill. This seed drill had great disks, actually double disks which allowed me to plant in many soil conditions. The scrapers worked great so that I could plant in moist soil for good germination and sprouting. You could set this seed drill for precise planting, getting just the right amount of seed and with new springs, the depth was correct all the way across the seed drill. Now the crops came up evenly and grew correctly.

We are all planting seed all the time in peoples' lives. The question is whose seed are we planting and are we seeing them come up and grow to a harvest? As seed planters, our seed drills need to be working properly so when the conditions are right to sow into someone's life, we won't plant too deep or too shallow. All the parts of our seed drills, ourselves, need to be in tune with God through the power of the Holy Spirit to know when, how, how much, what kind, where, and whatever else the Holy Spirit instructs us to do.

As we look at ourselves sometimes we have neglected maintaining our seed drills. Maybe we need to look more closely in the owner's manual, the Bible, and reestablish ourselves with the word of God to be a more effective planter. Go get out your grease gun and some new parts or, maybe even, ask for the means, the power, to become a whole new planter and just watch for the harvest to come.

Your brother in Christ Jesus,

Frankie

Hosea 10:12...Sow for yourselves righteousness, reap the fruit of unfailing love and break up your unplowed ground for it is time to seek the Lord, until He comes and showers righteousness on you.

Psalms 107:37...They sowed fields and planted vineyards that yielded a fruitful harvest.

Jeremiah 4:3...Break up your unplowed ground and do not sow among thorns.

Colossians 3:9 & 10...Do not lie to each other, since you have taken off your old self with its practices, and have put on the new self, which is being renewed in knowledge in the image of its creator.

05/01/03

Are You Wearing Asbestos?

In the last 10 to 15 years there has been a lot of hoopla about asbestos. There have been lawsuits, government mandates, and sicknesses, tearing down, cleaning up, and disposing of this product. It had many excellent uses like insulation, siding, fire retardants, etc. It can withstand tremendous heat, fire, and cold and is very weather resistant. The only problem is when the fine particles of the asbestos come in contact with the skin or is inhaled; it can cause problems in your body.

I was thinking about this and the fact is it is so fire resistant that fire can't get through it. John said that Jesus would baptize you with the Holy Spirit *and* with fire. The Bible tells us that God is love and also an all-consuming fire. The Bible also tells that we will be purified like fire purifies silver and gold. Maybe if we are continuing to make the same mistakes over and over, getting mad about the same thing, being jealous of the same things over and over, and following the way of unrighteousness, then just maybe we are wearing a coat made out of asbestos. The baptism of fire that burns or cleans the things off that are not of God can't get through the coat of asbestos. The problem is if we don't take off the coat, the hard shell of asbestos not only hinders the work of the fire of the Holy Spirit, but also locks in the things that are not of God. This could be sin and as we all know the wages of sin is death. This could be spiritual death or even fleshly death and illnesses.

Let us all search our hearts and look and see what kind of coat we are wearing and ask Jesus to baptize us with the Holy Spirit and with fire.

Your brother in Christ Jesus,

Frankie Jones

Malachi 3:2

......*For He is like a refiner's fire and like a launders soap.*

Hebrews 12:29

For our God is a consuming fire.

6/16/200

CHARLIE'S HAY CUTTER

Years ago, Charlie Baumer and his father, Laurie, cut and baled hay for many people in our canyon. Charlie had a self-propelled "Heston" hay cutter that could put down a lot of feed in a hurry. One year it had some mechanical difficulty that the mechanics just couldn't fix. Even the factory representatives couldn't seem to figure out the problem. They ended up putting a new hydraulic pump on the cutter, but to no avail the problem continued.

There was not enough power to the header to cut a full swath of feed at the correct speed. I felt so bad for them because in hay season everyone's hay seems to get ready all at once and they are anxiously waiting for their time to harvest.

One night after visiting with Charlie, I had a kind of vision or dream where I could see what the problem was. I thought I could help fix the problem. All kinds of things went through my mind, like, they will just think I am being a smart aleck or who do you think you are, and you'll look like a fool if you're not right.

The next day I went by Laurie and Charlie's house and told the story and asked if I could take a look. They said, "Sure, at this point we're ready for anything." I crawled under the cutter and had Charlie move the engaging lever back and forth. Just like I saw in my vision, the pin that connected the two pieces together was worn and also the holes in the shaft were worn. A quick adjustment and the problem was fixed. Charlie was exuberant and quickly began his work of harvesting again.

I'm telling you this story because I didn't realize that this was the Holy Spirit using me to bless someone else. At the time, I probably thought that I was just pretty smart. Now that I am older and have let the Spirit of Truth come into my heart, I realize that God cares about everything in our lives. Nothing is too big or too small for God. I believe it is when we can be obedient in the little things in our lives and trust in God, stepping out boldly when He tells us something, then He will begin to entrust you with carrying out His plan more and more.

Maybe we need to learn to trust God for a small mechanical gift before we can trust Him for a supernatural spiritual gift, such as healing or a prophecy or a word of knowledge. What is God through His Holy Spirit leading and guiding you to do? Are you listening? Can you hear?

>   Your brother in Christ Jesus,
>   Frankie

John 14:16,17

And I will ask the Father, and he will give you another Counselor, who will never leave you. He is the Holy Spirit, who leads into all truth. The world at large cannot receive him, because it isn't looking for him and doesn't recognize him. But you do, because he lives with you now and later will be in you.

John 14:26
But when the Father sends the Counselor as my representative – and by the Counselor I mean the Holy Spirit – he will teach you everything and will remind you of everything I myself have told you.

John 16: 13
When the Spirit of truth comes, he will guide you into all truth. He will not be presenting his own ideas; he will be telling you what he has heard. He will tell you about the future.

12/30/02

Dear Jesus

Dear Jesus, at church one day, Pastor Kent said if you had someone that touched your life, like a teacher, friend, or whoever, write them a note and let them know what they meant to you. As soon as he finished this statement, I thought about some of my teachers that were so important to me, like Max Amann, my agriculture teacher. Then I thought where would I stop writing people, like my parents and my grandparents that had so much to do with my life. My friends and their parents, my closest friends now and my newest friends that I share so many spiritual things of my life with. My children, my treasures in life, for which with their mother, I would do anything for.

But most of all, I think that I would like to just drop you a note, Jesus, to say thank you for coming into this world to teach us how to live; how to love; how to have compassion;

how to pray; how to treat people around us; and so much more. Thank you for suffering and dying on the cross for me, thank you that in doing this, I can have salvation, health, and healing. Thank you that you arose from the dead, conquering death so that I can live with you in eternity. Thank you that when you ascended to the right hand of the Father in heaven, you asked the Father and He sent the Holy Spirit, the comforter to be with me always.

Jesus, I want to thank you that through the Holy Spirit I can receive you and begin to walk in your ways to be empowered to do your will in my life. You are an awesome God and I just hope I can put a little smile on your face.

Love,

Frankie

08/12/2001

Do You Have a Crack in Your Caulk?

While taking down walls and baseboards in our church building, I noticed that around the return air ducts there was some rot and damage to part of the structure. Even though it wasn't a big part, the problem needed to be corrected before replacing everything new or the same problem would continue to cause rot even though it wouldn't be seen on the outside. Pastor Robert went outside and found that the caulk was dried out and cracked, letting water leak into the inside.

Through this the Lord showed me that when we get cracks in our armor, we leak and things of the world can come in and begin to cause internal damage even though we have our feet on the Rock, Jesus. As we grow in the Lord, we need to continue to turn our lives over to Him in all areas so that our temples are strong and whole without rot that can cause us to crumble. We need to continue to ask to be filled because when we are full and overflowing, life flows out and the things of the world can't get in.

So what will we do when we have injury or rot? Ask Jesus to fill you with the Holy Spirit and ask the Holy Spirit to reveal to you where the cracks are in your armor. Then seal them up with repentance, forgiveness, and the caulk of the word of God that brings the resurrection power of Jesus Christ into our lives.

Your brother in Christ,

Frankie Jones

Matthew 7:24 & 25

Therefore whoever hears these sayings of Mine, and does them, I will liken him to a wise man who builds his house on the rock. And the rain descended, the floods came, and the winds blew and beat on that house, and it did not fall for it was founded on the rock.

Feed My Sheep

All my life I've been feeding cattle on our ranch. While watching a newborn calf nurse its mother, I realized how dependent the calf's survival depended on its mother. All the calf had to do is just lay around and wait on its mother to nudge it up, lick it a little, and receive what its mother had for him. Sometimes the calf will just bawl a little and the mother will come running to protect or feed the calf again. As it grows older, the calf becomes more independent and the mother moves on to other pastures farther away, but not ever leaving the calf completely. Sooner or later, she or the rancher will wean the calf from dependence and it becomes part of the herd or another herd, thus being thrust into its purpose or plan for its life.

This is so much like what our Heavenly Father does with our lives. When we receive Jesus as our personal savior, we are born again. Being newborn, we are cared for constantly, loved, fed, and nurtured. When we are in trouble He is there, when we are hungry

He feeds us, when we are sick He heals us. But just like the calf, as we get older in our faith, God expects us to grow in our knowledge and wisdom and our understanding of Him. Our faith must grow and that comes from hearing the word of God and being obedient. We begin to understand what relationship, omnipresent and omnipotent means to us. Through the power of the Holy Spirit, we begin to get a glimpse of Thy Kingdom come on earth, as it is in heaven.

We are finding ourselves weaned off of baby food and moving on to become more mature Christians and thrust into His plan, our destiny that God has for us in the body of Christ. We begin to feed others while we are being fed.

Your Brother in Christ,

Frankie Jones

Hebrews 5:12-14

In fact, though by this time you ought to be teachers, you need someone to teach you the elementary truths of God's word all over again. You need milk, not solid food! Anyone, who lives on milk, being still an infant, is not acquainted with the teaching about righteousness. But solid food is for the mature, who by constant use have trained themselves to distinguish good from evil.

Ephesians 4:11-13

It was he who gave some to be apostles, some to be prophets, some to be evangelists, and some to be pastors and teachers, to prepare God's people for works of service, so that the body of Christ may be built up until we all reach unity in the faith and in the knowledge of the Son of God and become mature attaining to the whole measure of the fullness of Christ

John 21:15-18

Paraphrased by Frankie, Jesus says, "Simon if you love me, feed my lambs, care for my sheep, feed my sheep.

2/21/2002

For Men Only

Looking over our congregation Sunday, I was saddened to see very few young couples, very few children, and many wives with no husbands with them. I asked God, "what is wrong with this picture?" First, the Holy Spirit let me know right off that it is not the preacher. For example, we have had pastors that were so popular we had to have two services and pastors with only a houseful for one service. Why is this? I believe that we only want to be entertained and be ministered to. So when different pastors with different abilities come, so goes our attendance.

Men, what does that say about our professions of faith in our Lord and Savior Jesus Christ? I believe that we are breaking our covenant we made not only with our church, with our promise to support our church with our tithe, presence, and service, but also, with our covenant with Jesus Christ.

When we accept or ask Jesus to come into our lives, He comes into us and we into Him. At this time, whenever it may be, he brings the Holy Spirit with Him. This is when we have the availability of the realities of the Holy Spirit, for example, comforter, teacher, enabler, exciter, power giver, inspirer, guide, and many more. The Holy Spirit is the one that reveals the truths in scripture and lets us know what we should be doing in our lives.

One of these truths is that we (men) have been appointed to be heads of our family whether it is a family of one or more. Just as Christ is head of the church or Body of Christ, Ephesians 5, it is our commission to be the spiritual leaders in our family, which includes not neglecting church duties.

I believe that the spiritual awareness of our families should be the <u>number one priority</u> in our families and should not fall always on the women's backs, but thank God for faithful women, Ephesians 5:25. We should be able to give of ourselves like Christ gave of Himself for the church. God calls us to bring our families into the knowledge and wisdom of the saving grace of Jesus Christ until they make their own decisions about receiving Jesus Christ into their lives.

Be assured that each person is important in the Body of Christ, and when one part is missing, the whole body suffers.

If this letter is speaking to you like it is to me, don't let pride stand in your way of being obedient to what the Holy Spirit is telling you to do. I believe the Holy Spirit has given me the inspiration to write this letter, hopefully, to strengthen the Body of Christ in our church.

Your brother in Christ,

Frankie Jones

P.S. *To the women that couldn't help from reading this letter, please see that your spouse reads it, too. Thanks.*

For the husband is the head of the wife as Christ is the head of the church, his body, of which he is Savior. (Ephesians 5:23)

Husbands, love your wives, just as Christ loved the church and gave himself up for her.
(Ephesians 5:25)

Parables of a Rancher's Life   Frank W. Jones III

Gathering Angora Goats

For many years Dad and Jesse McFadin ran angora goats on our ranch. I loved working with goats and had a small herd of my own.

Twice a year we would have the goats sheared to sell the mohair. There was a lot of work involved in this process because in those days, we had a problem with screwworms. For a few weeks after they were shorn, each day we would gather them from off the mountains to check them for screwworms and bring them into a barn to protect them from the elements of weather like rain, hail, and cold.

Many times while gathering the goats there would be storms. We would work our way up the mountains, where the view was great, but there would be other times that the weather would be treacherous.

Northern(s) seem colder; thunderstorms louder; lightening more terrifying; and the rain more intense. Sometimes we would have to seek temporary shelter, then continue, but usually just pressed on to gather the goats so they wouldn't pile up on each other, trampling and suffocating each other.

I have heard, and even said myself, that after experiencing a mountain top experience with God that we have to go back down to the valley to reality. However, I now believe that is wrong. When God calls us to the mountain top and we experience Him and seek Him, we need not lose that relationship, that closeness, because He never moves from us, we only move from Him. Oh yes, the storms of life are violent on top of the mountain and sometimes we must hide in the cleft of the rocks until they pass. Sometimes we just have to stand our ground and trust in God to sustain us on the mountain and always we need to press on towards the goal of an eternal relationship with our Lord and savior, Jesus Christ.

We would bring the goats off the mountain like we also come off from the mountain top experience, whatever the reality. The truth is the experience the relationship with God through Jesus never leaves us because He places the Holy Spirit within us and abides with us. Psalms 23 says, in part, that even though I walk through the valley of death, I will fear no evil for Thou art with me. Amen.

Your brother in Christ,

Frankie

1 Corinthians 9:24,25

Do you not know that in a race all the runners run, but only one gets the prize? Run in such a way as to get the prize. Everyone who competes in the games goes into strict training. They do it to get a crown that will not last; but we do it to get a crown that will last forever.

1 Corinthians 10:12,13

So, if you think you are standing firm, be careful that you don't fall! No temptation has seized you except what is common to man. And God is faithful; he will not let you be tempted beyond what you can bear. But when you are tempted, he will also provide a way out so that you can stand up under it.

Psalm 27:5

For in the day of trouble he will keep me safe in his dwelling; he will hide me in the shelter of his sacred tent and set me high upon a rock.

Going in the Survival Cave

Many years ago my brother and his family, Shan, Nancy, Christy, and Lee, and Darlene, Robert, Amy, and I decided to spend an afternoon in what we call the survival cave on the ranch. We all entered the cave, some excitedly and some cautiously. We carried flashlights and lanterns in to provide plenty of light because deep inside the cave is total darkness.

This cave has many dangerous places that if the light goes out you probably couldn't get out without serious injury. This cave has hidden rooms and passages and at the end of two rooms there is a natural well with clear flowing water in the bottom about 30 feet deep. The only problem is that you would have to let yourself down on a rope to get a drink.

We decided to let the kids see how dark total darkness was, so we turned the lights off. You couldn't even see your hand right in front of your face. No one seemed to be too frightened, because we knew that we had the lights to show us the way out. As we began to get close to the entrance, you could see the natural light that revealed the outside world. There was only one problem, a barking lizard between the entrance and us was barking and barking, which terrified Christy, the youngest. She was not going to get out of the darkness to the light because of fear of the unknown. She didn't know what a barking lizard was and couldn't see it. She finally put her trust in her mother and father and saw the rest of us pass safely and then came out into the light of the outside world.

Isn't this a lot like our lives when we are living in darkness knowing there is light, but afraid to step into it because of fear of the unknown. Fear of a barking lizard in our ears telling us lies and deceiving us.

Jesus tells us that the light He has for us is great and abundant, but Satan tries to rule the carnal world and tells us differently. He tells us to stay in darkness, that he will provide us a light even though it will burn out. He tells us that there is plenty of water, but it won't quench our thirst.

As we come close to the entrance of our cave, our world, our lives, let us not be afraid to walk by the barking lizards and receive what Jesus has for us. Let's be sure not to neglect helping someone else pass by the barking lizards into the light of their salvation through Jesus Christ.

Your brother in Christ Jesus,

Frankie

John 8:12

…Jesus said to the people, "I am the light of the world. If you follow me, you won't be stumbling through the darkness, because you will have the light that leads to life."

John 12:46

…"I have come as a light to shine in this dark world, so that all who put their trust in me will no longer remain in the darkness."

Acts 26:18

…"to open their eyes so they may turn from darkness to light and from the power of Satan to God. Then they will receive forgiveness for their sins and be given a place among God's people, who are set apart by faith in me."

01/06/03

Going on a Deer Survey

At Bear Creek Ranch each year we run a deer survey. We do this by establishing a path where we count deer using the same path each year at approximately the same time of year. We drive along at night using spotlights counting and identifying each deer by sex (doe or buck), age (fawn or adult), or unidentifiable. When completed we add up the categories separately and compositely to determine density, doe/buck ratio, and percent fawn crop. The reason that we do this is to try to manage the deer harvest to maintain an ample amount of does and bucks with a high percentage fawn crop to replace those harvested and lost to natural causes, like predation, age, fences, auto collision, disease, and weather. This is to keep deer from getting so overpopulated that you have high risk to disease and starvation.

One year, one of my neighbors asked me to help run a deer survey to determine a reasonable harvest. We ran the survey and saw only a few deer. He later asked me my recommendation. I asked him how many deer he saw early in the morning and late afternoon and he said only a few. I told him, "I'm sorry to tell you, but if we didn't see them at night and you didn't see them in the day, you don't have enough for a harvest. You need to let them reestablish and get some age on them and then you will be ready for the harvest."

He asked what could have happened to them. I told him that they were taken from your possession by predation of other animals, disease, and over hunting and it destroyed his population.

So it is with our Christian living, if we aren't producing any fruit, we must not have any to give. If people don't see any fruit, we must not be bearing any. If we aren't seeing a harvest in our lives, we must not be sowing good seed or our fruit is bad fruit. From the abundance of our hearts our mouth speaks and our physical bodies act and react. *John 10:10 says... the thief comes only to steal and kill and destroy; I have come that they may have life, and have it to the full.* We must become imitators of Christ Jesus and when He abides in us and us in Him, we will produce good fruit that can be seen, heard, and experienced through relationship with our fellow man. In all things, walk in the fruits of the Holy Spirit: love, joy, peace, patience, kindness, long suffering, and gentleness.

                      Your brother in Christ Jesus,

                      Frankie Jones

10/20/2001

Matthew 7:16

By their fruit you will recognize them. Do people pick grapes from thorn bushes, or figs from thistles?

Colossians 3:5-15

Rules for Holy living.

Going Shrimping

As a child, we would go to the coast every summer for vacation to fish, swim, and visit kinfolk. A few times I was able to go shrimping with my aunt's dad, J.D. It was always exciting to drag the net, pull it up, and see what the catch would be. I always enjoyed listening to J. D. talk on the radio to his wife back home at the bait stand. They had kind of a code language to communicate how the catch was coming and if he needed more ice for the catch.

When we would pull the net in there would be all kinds of desirable and undesirable fish along with the shrimp in the net. The sorting would then begin to separate the good from the bad. There would be many hard head catfish, small uneatable fish, and jellyfish that would be thrown out and we would keep the good fish, like flounder, black drum, and most importantly, the shrimp. All sizes, small for bait and large for eating, were kept. The harvest of the sea is fascinating, yet all that was brought in was not kept, only the desirable was brought in to the store and kept.

The recent events this year have reminded me that there are many undesirable people on the earth today. God loves all of us like all of the things in the sea; however, He only accepts those that become His through Jesus Christ, those that become shrimp.

All you have to do is just ask, believe, and tell someone that you are a child of God.

In the end God will pull his net in and bring all of us in for the harvest. What will each one of us be? A hard head? A spiny fish? A jelly fish? A ribbon fish? Or a shrimp? Which way will God sort us? Will we be kept in the storehouse? The kingdom of heaven? Or thrown into the fiery furnace? Unlike the catch in the shrimping net that didn't have much of a choice; we have that choice to make a decision for Jesus before God pulls his net in. Let us not miss this season of harvest in our life because none of us know when our time on earth will cease.

                                      Your brother in Christ Jesus,

                                      Frankie

Matthew 13:47-50

Once again, the kingdom of heaven is like a net that was let down into the lake and caught all kinds of fish. When it was full the fishermen pulled it up on the shore. Then they sat down and collected the good fish in baskets, but threw the bad away. This is how it will be at the end of the age. The angels will come and separate the wicked from the righteous and throw them into the fiery furnace, where there will be weeping and gnashing of teeth.

10/07/2001

Going up in the Hemisphere Tower

Back in 1972, I was teaching vocational agriculture in Goliad, Texas. I was a young, 23 year old man just starting to learn about life and its many facets. I was a country boy and knew nothing of the city. Well that year the Young Farmer's Association had a convention in San Antonio at the Hemisphere Convention Center. I was lost before I even got started, but somehow with direction I made a few correct turns and ended up in the correct parking lot. I knew it was the right one because of the Hemisphere Tower.

When the meeting was over I knew that I needed to go south to Highway 181. I was confused and didn't know which way to go, so I thought that if I could just see where I was and where I needed to go or how to get there I would be on the right path. So I walked over to the tower, paid my dollar and went up to the observation deck. There I could see where I was; where I needed to go; how to get there; and where it would take me. After coming down, I got on the right roads and found my way home.

I had been to San Antonio many times before with other people, even to the Hemisphere area, but never on my own. When I stood on my own with all the hustle and bustle of the city and life, I realized I was lost and needed to find my way.

Sometimes it takes the hustle and bustle of life, the pain, problems, and attention that a crowd creates to stir our souls to seek the Lord. We can go to the alter of life with people all our life and not find the path home because in a crowd you just follow the crowd and you will go where they are going, however it might not be home. It is when we stand alone that we realize we are lost and need to seek a path, a direction to make it home. Sometimes we need to go up on a mountain, a tower, a tree to see Jesus, because the crowd of life has clouded our view.

In Luke 19:1-10, Zacchaeus had to climb up in a sycamore tree to see Jesus, to find his way to salvation, to be born again. What did or what will you have to do to find Jesus to find you way home?

Your brother in Christ,

Frankie

John 3:16

"For God so loved the world that He gave His only begotten Son, that whoever believes in Him should not perish but have everlasting life."

Romans 10:9 & 13

... that if you confess with your mouth the Lord Jesus and believe in your heart that God raised Him from the dead, you will be saved. For "whoever calls on the name of the Lord shall be saved."

05/03/02

HARVESTING DAVID'S WHEAT

After such a dry year last year, we were blessed with a wet fall, winter, and spring. It was a great year for oats and wheat and to those who had the faith to plant them after such a long, dry spell. Every day while driving by David Long's wheat field, I would be amazed at how quickly it was growing. It was growing so much that the few cows that were in the field couldn't keep the wheat grazed down. I asked David if he would like to harvest the wheat on the shares if I did all the work, to include re-cleaning for planting. He said yes that would be good.

When the wheat started heading out, I would pray blessings and productivity over the field when passing by. It hailed all around and the wind blew, but the field was spared. I noticed as the wheat matured that a weed, called prairie coneflower, started to come up and invade the weaker part of the field. I decided to go ahead and combine the entire field, weeds and all, bring in the grain, weed seed, and chaff to the bin, then re-clean the seed and purify it for planting.

In re-cleaning the seed, I ran it back through the combine where the fans create a strong airflow through the shakers and screens. The heavy, pure seed drops through and the light weed seed and chaff blow out the back. Then I burned the weed seed and chaff so they wouldn't spread in the pasture. The wheat was then ready for planting for the next crop.

While reading Luke 3:15-17, God's word says that Jesus will baptize with the Holy Spirit and fire. He will bring us into the threshing floor, separate us from the chaff with a winnowing fork and purify us with fire and burn up the chaff, the weed seed, and the undesirable things in us or among us.

I believe when we ask Jesus to come into our lives and give ourselves to Him through the power of the Holy Spirit, He will begin the process of re-cleaning or separating the undesirable things out of our lives and He will get rid of these things with the unquenchable fire of the Holy Spirit.

Being a farmer and rancher, I know that you don't want to plant bad seed or breed up inferior livestock. I pray that we will allow Jesus to use this winnowing fork on us so that the body of Christ will function properly and effectively through the power of the Holy Spirit.

Your brother in Christ,

Frankie

8/11/2001

How to Sprout a Mountain Laurel Seed

Have you ever seen a mountain laurel bush in spring bloom? It is a gorgeous sight of purple and white blooms with a sweet smelling fragrance. They seem to be everywhere especially if you don't really want them. But to plant mountain laurel seeds and get them to sprout is not an easy thing. In nature, they fall off in a pod or bust out and fall on the ground. The outer shell is very hard and durable, withstanding elements of nature for years before conditions are just right before they sprout. Sometimes, they go through the digestive system of an animal, or cracked washing down a creek. Sometimes man will stimulate them by burning or doing brush work with mechanical equipment, like a bulldozer. It is when you think they will be destroyed the seed germinates, takes root, and develops into a beautiful plant that is very hardy and then will begin to produce fruit.

I believe many of us are like a mountain laurel seed in that we must be weathered down and exposed to the elements of life before we can take root and sprout. Some of us have to be cracked or broken because our outer shell is too thick and hard. We have to be planted over and over, exposed and re-exposed to the elements of life before we will come to Jesus and ask Him to be Lord of our lives. However, when we finally take root in Jesus, He will manifest a beautiful person with a new heart that will produce good fruit and be a blessing to God and those we come in contact with.

We must continue to plant seeds of fruit in Jesus Christ to all we come in contact with.

The other day my son, Robert, said, "Dad, don't give up and don't get discouraged. You and Mom planted seeds in me for 28 years before you saw the harvest." He knows what I'm writing about because he was one that had to be weathered severely, cracked, and finally broken before he could sprout.

I pray that none of us have to be cracked or broken before we call on Jesus for salvation, but I am so thankful for the beauty and hardness of a mountain laurel bush and its seeds.

Remember this:

Whoever sows sparingly will also reap sparingly, and whoever sows generously will also reap generously. (2 Corinthians 9:6)

In bringing many sons to glory, it was fitting that God, for whom and through whom everything exists, should make the author of their salvation perfect through suffering. (Hebrews 2:10)

Therefore Jesus said again, "I tell you the truth, I am the gate for the sheep. All who ever came before me were thieves and robbers, but the sheep did not listen to them. I am the gate; whoever enters through me will be saved. He will come in and go out, and find pasture. The thief comes only to steal and kill and destroy; I have come that they may have life, and have it to the full. (John 10:7-10)

Frank Jones III

Huntin' in Colorado

Have you ever been huntin' in Colorado? I have, but not until I had heard about it for many years first. I call it huntin' because hunting sounds a little sissy like. As a child, I saw my dad, Sid, Everett, Les, Hilmer, Hubert, and many more go huntin' in Colorado. They would tell stories over and over each year, show pictures, movies, and talk about the trophies hanging on their walls.

It wasn't long before we all knew about Bear Basin, Suicide Ridge, the Rock, Shaw Creek, Bear Creek, Hosick, Winnemanueche, Meadows, and Down Timbers. We heard stories of their experiences in all of these places. Stories like the one that got away, deep snow, how every time Everette shot something, it would be full of holes. How they tracked an elk for miles. How Hilmer unloaded his gun on a huge elk never firing a shot from the excitement.

It was like I had been there. I knew what it looked like. I knew where it was. I knew all about the experience, and even thought I had experienced it from just knowing and talking to people that had really been there and hunted in Colorado before. But, the truth was I hadn't, but finally it was my turn. It was great, even better than I could have ever expect or imagine. Now I have my own experiences, stories, and relationships that developed from making the step to say I want to go, I need to go, I am going, and I went.

This experience is so much like my experience and relationship with Jesus. For many years, I heard about Abraham, Moses, David, Jesus, and other stories in the Bible, over and over for years, watching movies on television, Sunday school, sermons, revivals, and parables. I participated in plays about the birth of Christ Jesus, sang songs, plays about the crucifixion and many others. I joined the church, was baptized as a baby, and I guess, I thought that I had experienced Jesus the Savior, the living Christ, but I hadn't.

I lacked the most important part, asking Jesus to come into my life, my heart and receiving Him and developing a personal relationship with Him. But, I did and now I have my own stories of what Jesus is doing in my life that I want to share with people.

Have you ever been huntin' in Colorado? Do you have a personal relationship with Jesus the living Savior? Isn't it your turn?

> With love from your brother in Christ,
>
> Frankie

2/21/2002

Killing Brush

Being ranchers, we are always engaged in brush control. One way we attempt to control brush is by the use of chemicals. It is very important to read the labels to administer the right amount of chemical to the species of brush at the right time and by the correct method.

Mountain laurel and cactus are two plants that invade our ranch and need to be controlled so that it won't spread to the point where the land is not productive. As ranchers, we need to grow grass so we must kill certain species so the grass can grow and the cattle can be fed by eating the grass.

Some brush needs to be saturated in the chemical so that each leaf will take the chemical to the root. Some brush only takes a few drops of chemical on the trunk or just on the ground and the root will absorb it killing the plant.

So it is with baptism. I know people worry about how to be baptized. I believe that how isn't the important part, but that the water and the Spirit get to your heart.

When the chemical gets to the root the plant dies. So it is with our flesh, we can be immersed or we can be sprinkled, but if it doesn't get to the heart or come from the heart, flesh won't die. When our flesh dies, God can draw near to us. He can come close. It is up to us how much flesh, our own desires or things of the world, will control us. I saw a bumper sticker once that said, "Let go and let God." Less of self means more of God.

Your brother in Christ,

Frankie

John 3:3

In reply Jesus declared, "I tell you the truth, no one can see the kingdom of God unless he is born again."

John 3:5-6

Jesus answered, "I tell you the truth, no one can enter the kingdom of God unless he is born of water and the Spirit. Flesh gives birth to flesh, but the Spirit gives birth to spirit."

John 5:24

"I tell you the truth, whoever hears my word and believes him who sent me has eternal life and will not be condemned; he has crossed over from death to life."

Romans 8:13-14

For if you live according to the sinful nature, you will die; but if by the Spirit you put to death the misdeeds of the body, you will live, because those who are led by the Spirit of God are sons of God.

12/19/2001

Late Winter Burn

Every year in February and March we burn off some of our pastures to help stimulate new growth and rid the pastures of things like little cedar and old grass growth that has become coarse and so fibrous that nothing will eat it. This old grass has no food value and the brush species need to be burned back so the new, fresh, and nutritious plants will thrive. This new growth is tender and rich in nutrients, which attracts bugs, birds, wildlife, and livestock. This is a tool of pasture management that is very effective and effects plants and animals alike.

I believe that when we open our hearts to the cleansing fire of the Holy Spirit and let Him burn off the chaff, the calluses, the hardness, and the veils, we become new, fresh and attractive. We want to grow, we are stimulated, excited, and it shows. People can see this in you and you don't have to say much, all you have to do is just shine.

Be renewed in Jesus and let His light shine through you. Be a beacon in someone's darkness, introduce someone to the saving grace of Jesus Christ.

Your brother in Christ,

Frankie

Ezekiel 36:25-27

" Then I will sprinkle clean water on you, and you shall be clean; I will cleanse you from all your filthiness and from all your idols.
"I will give you a new heart and put a new spirit within you; I will take the heart of stone out of your flesh and give you a heart of flesh.
"I will put My Spirit within you and cause you to walk in My statues, and you will keep My judgments and do them."

Acts 13:47

"For so the Lord has commanded us:
I have set you as a light to the Gentiles, that you should be for salvation to the ends of the earth."

Luke 8:16

"No one, when he has lit a lamp, covers it with a vessel or puts it under a bed, but sets it on a lampstand, that those who enter may see the light."

02/20/02

Learning to Swim

This past summer my wife, Darlene, decided to take some time to help my Granddaughter Chase learn to swim. She knew a little from last year, but because of the drought and everybody's schedule she didn't get to go enough to learn. As Darlene began to take her, she would put on her "floaties" and swim in the shallow end while the other kids would be swimming in the deep end and jumping off the diving board. Every now and then, they would come into the shallow and play games and try to include her. But her fear would overtake her and she would retreat back to the shallow.

Darlene just kept on taking her and being there for her with gentle nudges but not scaring her. The main thing that drew her to swim in the deep and test her ability was the activity of the other children. Chase would think, "Well, if they can do that, I can." The more she saw them swim and not sink, she slowly decided that she *could* do it! In no time at all, she was jumping in the pool off the diving board and swimming completely on her own, not realizing that the water was holding her up.

So it is with our Christian walk with Jesus. We get in the water not really knowing what to do even though we have heard it over and over from preachers, teachers, friends, and the word of God. The lure or tugging of the heart comes from Jesus gently calling us to take the first step into salvation. We see our friends basking in the love of Jesus, wanting to get in, but afraid to take off our floaties, our pride. Sometimes we get scared because of something we don't understand, so we back off, but Jesus keeps nudging us forward. He gives us the rulebook or the road map if we will just read and study it as we go along, asking Him for directions, and we will get into a new level of faith.

As we grow, we will begin to want to share with all believers and non-believers. Titles of places of worship don't seem to be as important, but people are more important.

Sometimes we just have to jump off the diving board and swim up for air and see what God has for us. We must remember that when swimming with Jesus streams of living water will support us because when we abide in Him and He with us, we become part of that living water.

Frankie Jones

John 15:5

"I am the vine; you are the branches. If a man remains in me and I in him, he will bear much fruit; apart from me you can do nothing."

John 7:39

"Whoever believes in me, as the Scripture has said, streams of living water will flow from within him."

9/24/2001

Lee Sellers Made a Difference

Going to school in Utopia was a very special time in my life like many others. There are many people that I remember but today while listening to a message on TV, I thought of Lee Sellers. Lee was our school custodian and bus driver for many years. He always had a smile and a kind word. When driving the bus, I remember that when Mom wasn't there to pick us up, he would wait or sometimes just take us all the way to the house. We knew he loved us by the way he showed us compassion. We never felt fear around him because of his size and manliness and never acting put out because we were slow or late. You might say the circumstances of the world never seemed to be an inconvenience to him. When we needed to get into the school because we forgot something he would go let us in. He had the keys to everything in the school and could go in anywhere he wanted or needed to, more so than the superintendent.

While reading Matthew, Jesus said that the son of man came not to be served but to serve and be a ransom for many. This reminded me of Lee Sellers where in the eyes of the world a custodian job might not be the job we would want to have, but it is like what Jesus was to us all even to the point of death. He was willing to clean up the messes of our lives.

Jesus is strong, manly, loving, compassionate, caring, patient, fearless, and is the key to the kingdom of God. He can go anywhere and do anything good anytime anywhere. Because He was a servant, doors were opened to have access to the hearts of man. So it was with Lee Sellers because he was a servant he had access to any room and any building on campus.

So let us all remember that it is when we are willing to become a servant, to wash someone's feet, that is when we are allowed to have access into someone's heart and to share the love of Jesus and his saving grace.

Your brother in Christ,

Frankie

Matthew 20:28

"just as the Son of Man did not come to be served, but to serve, and to give His life a ransom for many."

October 2002

Looking from the Mountain Top

The other day I was on top of the mountain filling up deer feeders. On the way down I stopped and was just giving thanks to God for such a beautiful creation as I looked over the canyons and streams that are located on our ranch. Then I noticed all of the roads and paths that go up and down the mountains across creeks and canyons and back to the highway or other destinations. After the flood this summer we worked hard to repair the roads that had been washed-out and eroded by the floodwaters. It was important to get them finished and passable because many hunters would be traveling the roads in only a short time.

There was also a beauty of the pastures, as the tall grass would wave with the wind. It seemed like a pillow of grass and would be easy to just drive around the washouts but that view was deceiving even though it looked inviting or interesting. So many times when we have driven off the road we have blown out a tire or bent a tie rod on a stump, which was hidden by the grass. We have even run into a hole, gotten stuck and had to get help to get out.

As I reflected on all this I was reminded that God tells us in his word, that the path is narrow and the gate is narrow to enter the kingdom of Heaven. Wide is the road to destruction.

So many times the things of the world look so important or so good; so enticing; so luring that our mind, our will, our emotions, and even our body wants to take that path for an infinite number of reasons. However, there are many hidden things that lead to our destruction, some little by little and some all at once. When we listen to God's spirit within us He will always lead us on the right path. God will go before us and repair all the washouts; remove all the fallen trees; and repair the roads so that we are able to stay

on His path that leads to eternal life with Him.

> Your brother in Christ,
> Frankie

Proverbs 2:8

He guards the paths of justice, and preserves the way of His saints.

Proverbs 4:14

Do not enter the path of the wicked, and do not walk in the way of evil.

Proverbs 8:32

"Now therefore, listen to me, my children, for blessed are those who keep my ways."

Matthew 7:13,14

"Enter by the narrow gate; for wide is the gate and broad is the way that leads to destruction, and there are many who go in by it. "Because narrow is the gate and difficult is the way which leads to life, and there are few who find it."

Luke 13:24,25

"Strive to enter through the narrow gate, for many, I say to you, will seek to enter and will not be able.
"When once the Master of the house has risen and shut the door, and you begin to stand outside and knock at the door, saying, 'Lord, Lord, open for us,' and He will answer and say to you, 'I do not know you, where you are from,'

John 10:7-9

Then Jesus said to them again, "Most assuredly, I say to you, I am the door of the sheep.
"All who ever came before Me are thieves and robbers, but the sheep did not hear them.
"I am the door. If anyone enters by Me, he will be saved, and will go in and out and find pasture."

November 2002

Looking Through the Lens of a Camera

This summer Ray Harp gave a talk at the men's breakfast and at one point mentioned the function of a camera. When you look through the eyepiece of a camera your eye catches the image that you want to capture. When you push the button on the camera the camera lens opens and light comes into darkness bringing the imprint of the image. This image is reflected off of a mirror turned upside down and placed on the film, the negative. While in the darkroom the negative is exposed to the processing solution and transposed or transfigured to the picture. What was in darkness and turned upside down is now made new, upright, and then slowly becomes a new image that is visible, bright, and recognizable.

I thought, wow, that is what Jesus does in our lives. We see the person Jesus wants us to be and even though we are in darkness when we open the lens to our heart and expose ourselves to the light, Jesus comes in and shows us what we need to be. This turns our life upside down because we are not the way we used to be. During this process the Holy Spirit begins to stir the very essence of our heart and soul. He begins to birth us into a new person, born again, turned upside down, and placed upright by the solution, the blood of Christ, with a new heart and renewed mind, an image that is the righteousness of God or you might say right with God. God has provided a way for us to be with Him now and eternally. Have you opened the lens to your heart and let Jesus come in to take over and make you a new lasting imprint that will never fade?

>Your brother in Christ,

>Frankie

John 3:3
I tell you the truth, no one can see the kingdom of God unless he is born again.

John 3:21
But whoever lives by the truth comes into the light, so that it may be seen plainly that what he has done has been done through God.

12/8/02

Managing Bear Creek Ranch
"A Father & Son"

I have been involved in agriculture all my life. Early in life I spent most of my time enjoying the creation of the ranch where I grew up. I never realized that my Dad was teaching me all the time as we worked and played. As I grew older my love for the land and the caring for it grew. The more I worked the more I learned, Dad always explaining why we did this and that at certain times of the year. He also taught me things without even telling me, about the importance of worship, community service, fellowship, and friends.

I went off to college, graduated and then taught agriculture for a few years. When returning to the ranch, I was excited and enthused, however, Dad slowly let me make more decisions as I proved worthy of the task one by one until he basically turned the operation over to me. I still go to him for advice and probably always will.

Dad realized that he must decrease in the decisions and responsibilities as I increased in them. He knew that he had instilled them in me and that I had even received new knowledge in some areas that he didn't have. To turn over an operation of a business or a way of life to a son brings joy to a father and makes him feel good about his life's work.

I believe that our life in Jesus Christ is a lot like this. Jesus teaches us about himself little by little until we become one with Him. As He increases in our life, we decrease in our hold on our old life in the world and begin to let Him take over ours. We are still ourselves, but the things that used to control us are not as important as who leads us. Let us all let Christ Jesus guide us in our lives.

Love in Christ,

Frankie

John 3:30

He must become greater and greater and I must become less and less.

10/26/2001

Mutt and Jeff

About 20 years ago, my good friend, Tom and I bought two mules. I never dreamed I would learn a valuable lesson 20 years later. We purchased these mules for hunting trips in Colorado for packing and riding. We worked diligently breaking and training these mules. Jeff seemed to become easier to break than Mutt, but Mutt was stronger, quicker with power steering, and a good travel gait.

Once after leading Mutt for several miles under full pack, Tom decided this would be a good time to ride him. Tom mounted Mutt and it seemed that all our training was in vain. Mutt bent his neck until his head was pulled all the way to his chest, then proceeded to run at will, out of control, in a large 75 acre field with Tom hanging on for dear life. Mutt made a large circle spotting a low limb and proceeded to unseat his loving rider and trainer. To say the least, as time passed after many trips hunting, Mutt seemed to prove untrustworthy for riding even though we could use him for packing.

Because of his lack of trustworthiness and his inability to be broken and molded into what we wanted of him, he was left behind or shelved.

Let us not be shelved or left behind by God because we would not be broken to the point where we can be molded into the person that God wants us to be. Being broken, we become a blessing to God for his service so that we might receive the blessings that He has for us.

Your brother in Christ,

Frankie Jones

My Cows Know My Voice

For years we gathered cattle with horses and dogs and had a lot of fun doing it that way. Now I use a completely different method of gathering cattle. I call them by their name, " suu cow." They hear my voice and just come running. This doesn't happen by coincidence, but by a lot of time developing a relationship with them. I start out by feeding them and soon they learn that I'm not a threat, but a reward. When gathering, we usually feed them; rid them of pests, like flies, ticks, and lice; vaccinate them to protect them from disease; treat them for sickness and healing; and/or direct them into their purpose in life. Some always come early; some only when they are hungry; some will stand outside the pen and watch for a while and then cautiously come in; and some will go in only when pushed and then are constantly trying to get back out. The ones that continually cause trouble usually get sold so they don't lead the others astray.

Jesus is calling us by our name into a personal relationship with him through the still small voice of the Holy Spirit. He is calling us for an eternal relationship with Him. However, in this relationship our faith should be growing. This happens by feeding, hearing the word of God; by reading the bible; preaching; prophesy; witnessing; testimonies; experiencing Jesus in our lives; miracles; and more.

Maybe Jesus is calling us to direct us into our purpose in life. Do you hear Jesus calling today? Are you going to come running? Are you hungry? Are you cautious and afraid? Are you running away from that call?

"I am the good shepherd; and I know My sheep and am known by My own. As the Father knows Me, even so I know the Father and I lay down My life for the sheep." (John 10:14-15).

"I still have many things to say to you, but you cannot bear them now. However, when He, the Spirit of truth, has come, He will guide you into all truth; for He will not speak on His own authority, but whatever He hears He will speak; and He will tell you things to come." (John 16:12-13).

So then faith comes by hearing, and hearing by the word of God. (Romans 10:17)

                Your brother in Christ,

                Frankie Jones

6/20/2001

My Linkage was Frozen Up

The other day I was working on our bulldozer engine. Older bulldozers have small starting engines used to start the main engine. This small engine has had no power for about two or three years, making it very hard to start the main engine. The small engine wouldn't start, so I removed the hood of the bulldozer so that I could see what was going on inside. After getting the small engine to start, I observed that when I would increase the throttle, the linkage to the governor would not move. I adjusted the tension and oiled the linkage where it was frozen up. This time the small engine throttled up to a high rpm with ample power to start the large engine.

One day while working, I was thinking about the frozen linkage and compared it to the Holy Spirit. I believe that sometimes we have let the Holy Spirit freeze up within us to the point where we have no power to be the person God wants us to be. I believe that when we free up the Holy Spirit in our lives that He will provide all we need to follow Jesus' commands in our lives. I had to take the hood off the bulldozer to identify the problem, but God sees in our heart and knows all our needs. If we will ask the Holy Spirit to mold us and empower us then I believe we will begin to operate in the purpose and will of God in our lives.

The frozen linkage was keeping me from starting the larger engine <u>so that</u> I could engage the bulldozer into the purposes that it was made for, like cleaning up pastures of unwanted brush, making roads, and building dams.

When we free up the Holy Spirit and invite Him in, He will convict us of the unwanted things in our lives, clean us up so that we can take a new road in life and bear fruit. He will also build dams or roadblocks in our life by revealing the truth about things in our lives that separate us from God.

As we seek God, let us all pray for the fruits and gifts of the Holy Spirit and search God's word for these attributes of the Holy Spirit.

"Behold, I send the Promise of My Father upon you; but tarry in the city of Jerusalem until you are endued with power from on high." (Luke 24:49)

"But when the Helper comes, whom I shall send to you from the Father, the Spirit of truth who proceeds from the Father, He will testify of Me." (John 15:26)

"Nevertheless I tell you the truth. It is to your advantage that I go away; for if I do not go away, the Helper will not come to you; but if I depart, I will send Him to you. And when He has come, He will convict the world of sin, and of righteousness, and of judgment:" (John 16:7-8)

Your Brother in Christ Jesus,

Frankie Jones

My Turbo Blew Off

One day while coming back from Beeville, I was pulling our 32 foot trailer with a hay cutter and tractor on it. It was a very heavy load but the 7.3 liter turbo powered diesel engine had plenty of power to deliver the load. Right out of Hondo, I heard a pop and the truck began to lose power to the point it would not pull the load. The engine would run and run smoothly, however it had no power. When I would engage the clutch the truck would bog down and could hardly move, it couldn't deliver the goods. What had happened is that the tube that delivers the turbo-pressured air to the engine blew off so that the engine lost the super power of the turbo. The extra power source was disconnected.

When we try to deliver our life's work on our own we will always run out of power. If we try to be a disciple of

Jesus Christ on our own we might give up, get worn out, get frustrated, and be unable to deliver the message, the gospel of Jesus Christ. We need to be like the disciples at Pentecost where Jesus told them to wait until they were empowered by the Holy Spirit.

We need to pray that Jesus baptize us with the Holy Spirit and with fire so that we will be supernaturally empowered to be his disciples. Like my truck we can run, we can even move ourselves around, but without the turbocharger, the Holy Spirit, we won't have the supernatural power to deliver the goods, the gospel of Jesus Christ. The power to bring hope where there seems to be no hope; to bring comfort where it seems there is no comfort; to bring salvation to the lost; to bring the healing power of Jesus' name to those that would believe; and to bring the message of deliverance to those in need.

On my truck, all I had to do was loosen up the clamp and reconnect the hose to the turbo. In our lives, all we have to do is loosen up our pride and ask the Holy Spirit to fill us and empower us to be disciples for Jesus Christ.

                                              Your brother in Christ,

                                              Frankie

Old Sunny

Years ago when I was a kid, Dad and Jess McFadin ran a lot of angora goats. Each year after shearing we would have to gather them each afternoon for several weeks until their hair would grow back some to protect them from cold rain. We always had some experienced horses, one named Sunny, and others that were young and not experienced, especially in traveling in rough, mountain terrain. Dad and Jess would ride Old Sunny and I would ride Lightening or Ginger, which were more spirited.

Going up the mountain, Old Sunny would take his time, rest a little, and carefully ease up the trail not using all of his energy just getting up the mountain because he knew what was ahead. However, Ginger wanted to run up the mountain showing off her strength and youth. By the time we made it up, she would be tired, but quickly recovered.

Old Sunny would work the ledges slowly and surely, being careful to put each step in a safe place to avoid slipping and sliding, but Ginger would prance around always slipping and being dangerous, however always learning as we traveled. When we got to the far end of the pasture and all we had to do was come off the mountain down the valley and pen the goats, we couldn't wait because we knew we could run free and feel the wind in our faces.

As I was following Dad and Old Sunny, all of a sudden I couldn't see any trail, all I could see was about 50 yards of steep, rocky ledges (solid rock). I said, "Dad, we can't go here, it is too steep and dangerous. I'll just go back around the way we came." He said, "No, it's late and will be dark before you get there. Just do what I do and follow me and I will show you the way through the steep and rough part."

He dismounted and unsnapped the reins on one side so he could get way out in front of Old Sunny and started down the mountain. Sunny practically sat down and slid all the way down with sparks flying in all directions, but never faltering because he had done it many times before and he trusted Dad not to lead him into danger. As Ginger and I watched, we were nervous and very humbled. Our youth, strength, and spiritedness weren't much help now. I stepped out and made the first step down the mountain, Ginger nervously following, sparks flying sliding down. We made it safely, so thankful that we had someone to set the example and show us the way. We mounted back up and loped across the valley, wind in our faces, full of confidence, ready for a new day.

Are we being Old Sunny for our brothers and sisters in Christ, for the unsaved, or lost? Are we there to see those around us through the steep, rocky times in their lives? Are we setting the examples for our friends and family? Are we leading the way and letting God use us as his priest to each other? Have we humbled ourselves, broken our pride, and called out to Jesus to lead us and be the Master of our lives? Jesus wants to be the Master of our lives and lead and guide us through life. Let us not pass up the chance for Jesus to take the reins of our journey. There is victory in Jesus.

Your brother in Christ,

Frankie Jones

Our Old Ranch Truck

A while back our old ranch truck gave us quite a shock. After being parked in the barn for a couple of weeks, I decided to crank it up and feed deer in it. It wouldn't start up, as a matter of fact, it wouldn't even turn over. So we charged the batteries real good, but to no avail. It would not start and we couldn't even move the engine by pulling the truck. It was like someone had thrown a crowbar into the engine.

All types of thoughts began to go through Lee's and my minds of what must have happened. We talked to my friend and mechanic, John T., and asked him if he would work on it. As we discussed it, all of the worst scenarios we could think of came up.

The truck needed a new clutch, so we decided we had better just pull the engine and find out how bad the damage really was. As John T. began to work on the engine, he pulled the exhaust manifolds off and corn started pouring out. It appeared as if a mouse, or a few mice, had packed the engine full of corn so that the pistons could not move. What a relief it was that the engine wasn't damaged, only locked up. It was fixed real easily.

This little incident sounds a lot like life when we let the things seen and imagined get out of control. The eyes and ears of the physical body can get the mind going out of control, thus making our body sick with fear. When this happens, we need to be renewed in our heart and soul so that our eyes and ears will get back in line with our spirit and make us complete again. We need healing spiritually and physically. Well guess what? Just like I called on John T. to fix my truck by looking inside the engine, Jesus sees all, inside and out and He can fix us up. All we have to do is ask and believe. Just like I turned that old ranch truck over to John T., we need to turn ourselves over to Jesus for the touch of the Master's hand.

>Your brother in Christ,
>
>Frankie

2 Corinthians 4:18
So we fix our eyes not on what is seen, but on what is unseen. For what is seen is temporary, but what is unseen is eternal.

Matthew 9:35
Jesus went through all the towns and villages, teaching in their synagogues, preaching the good news of the kingdom and healing every disease and sickness.

02/05/2002

Planting Klein Grass Seed

August 2002

About twenty-eight years ago Dad and I decided to plant Klein grass in most of our old fields. I didn't know too much about how to prepare the soil for such a tiny seed so I began to research about how much seed to plant, when, and how to plant it.

First, I prepared the soil by plowing and getting a fine seed bed free from weeds and other grasses. Then I planted about three pounds of pure live seed per acre about one-fourth of an inch deep. Afterwards I rolled the soil to pack it down and firm it up. All of these processes had to be done at the right time with the right equipment and the right moisture. Then all I had to do was just sit back and wait. Waiting was the hardest part of the job. I was used to having a crop of grazer being up in a week and growing rapidly, however, the Klein grass has its own timing. I would worry and look, dig and study, trying to determine if the seed was growing. My faith in the seed growing was wavering even to the point that I even re-plowed and replanted one field. A wise person told me to be patient, treat the field as if the seed was growing. So I sprayed the weeds and shredded the other competing grasses. I knew that the seed was good because it was certified PLS, which means that if it had a 75% germination you would get an extra 25% to make 100% pure live seed, viable, full of life, proven to stand the test. I knew the soil was prepared well, but I just wanted to see proof. *Now*.

How many times do we pray for things or people wanting everything to happen when and how we want them to? God's word tells us that there is a time and a season for everything. A time to prepare, a time to plant, a time to water or feed, a time to harvest. All these things come along in God's time even though we would really like to be in control. If I plant oats in the summer it won't sprout and if I plant grazer in the winter it won't sprout.

God has his own timing for His plan in our lives. Let us not be impatient and let us not miss God's timing in our lives. When He tells us to plant, then plant; to harvest then harvest; to feed then feed. Be obedient to what God is calling you to do. Don't miss the blessing He has for you or someone else that He wants you to bless.

Let us stand on God's promises, His word, it is life to our souls, it is the certified pure live seed.

Your brother in Christ,

Frankie

Ecclesiastes 3:1
To everything there is a season, A time for every purpose under heaven:.........

1Peter 1:24,25
... because "All flesh is as grass, And all the glory of man as the flower of the grass, The grass withers, And its flower falls away, "But the word of the Lord endures forever."

Pruning Fruit Trees

For as long as I can remember Dad always had fruit trees. Several different varieties, but my favorite was peach trees, probably because I like to eat them the most. In the winter Dad would prune the peach trees when they were dormant, not producing and with no leaves. He would shape the tree so that the limbs wouldn't get too long and break under the weight of the fruit. He would also prune in the center of the tree so the limbs could grow inward. In the spring from the new buds there would be new growth and from the new growth blooms and from the blooms fruit would be produced. When we didn't prune the trees would produce, but we never seemed to get a harvest. There would always seem to be a problem. A limb would break or the fruit would fall off or maybe not even have any fruit.

I never realized how much this is what God does in our lives as He prunes us. You see God knows that fruit, good fruit that will last, comes when we have growth and the pruning stimulates new growth. So He snips and cuts on our lives by means of the Holy Spirit convicting us of guilt in regard to sin in our lives so that we will be productive and strong even producing fruit during and after a storm. All we have to do is be the branches and stay hooked up to the trunk or, may I say, the vine, which is Jesus. Jesus tells us in His word that apart from Him we can do nothing. So let us abide in Jesus and let God prune us for His use in His kingdom.

Your brother in Christ,

Frankie

John 15:1-5

*"I am the true vine, and My Father is the vinedresser.
"Every branch in Me that does not bear fruit He takes away; and every branch that bears fruit He prunes, that it may bear more fruit.*

"You are already clean because of the word which I have spoken to you."Abide in Me, and I in you. As the branch cannot bear fruit of itself, unless it abides in the vine, neither can you, unless you abide in Me. "I am the vine, you are the branches. He who abides in Me, and I in him, bears much fruit; for without Me you can do nothing."

7/15/02

Singeing Doves

Growing up on a ranch, I had the opportunity to hunt with my dad. What great memories I have of going dove hunting with him from a small boy until now. One thing that I will never forget is that when it came to cleaning the birds, we were always required to pick them thoroughly because we didn't want to waste even the legs or the wings. So we have always picked the doves completely, nearly to the end of the wings. Mother had a gas burning stove and Dad would take the birds and put them over the fire a little at a time to burn off, or singe, the pinfeathers and fuzz, kind of like down, off the doves. Then we would cut down the back and remove the blood and entrails of the birds, washing them clean with water, then they would be ready for cooking.

As Christians, God, through the filling of the Holy Spirit into his children, is cleaning us up little by little, plucking the things out of our lives that separate us from Him. He is using Jesus to baptize us with the Holy Spirit and with fire to purify our hearts with His sanctifying grace so that we will be effective in the body of Christ. Jesus is using water for repentance and blood to wash away our sins to make us presentable to God, the Father.

Are we ready for cooking? To be purified by fire? To be placed in service to God through the body of Christ? Do you know your place in the body of Christ? Ask the Holy Spirit to teach you and reveal to you through His word what it is He wants of you, His plan for you, and may God be glorified. Amen.

Frankie Jones

Matthew 3:11

I baptize you with water for repentance, but after me will come one who is more powerful than I, whose sandals I am not fit to carry. He will baptize you with the Holy Spirit and with fire.

1 John 1:7 & 9

But if we walk in the light as he is in the light, we have fellowship with one another, and the blood of Jesus, his Son, purifies us from all sin.

If we confess our sins, he is faithful and just and will forgive us our sins and purify us from all unrighteousness.

Isaiah 6:6 & 7

Then one of the seraphs flew to me with a live coal in his hand, which he had taken with tongs from the altar. With it he touched my mouth and said, "See, this has touched your lips, your guilt is taken away and your sin atoned for."

Psalms 12:6

And the words of the Lord are flawless, like silver refined in a furnace of clay, purified seven times.

10/12/2001

Sowing Wild Oats

For years we have planted oats in the fall for grazing and a harvest of grain. One year when harvesting the grain, I noticed a black, furry grain mixed in with the good grain. The next year at planting time instead of buying new, clean, certified seed I planted the old seed. I prepared the soil properly, fertilized it, and it seemed to be a great crop. However, when I harvested the crop, it was full of black furry grain that was no good. The wild oats had practically choked out the good. The next year I had to wait and plow under the volunteer crop to kill out the wild oats and start out new with pure certified seed. Free from defective seed, the crop was good and the harvest was plentiful.

As Christians, we often do the preparation for seed planting to bring in a harvest for Jesus, but often the seeds don't come up or if they do, they don't take root and fade away. I wonder if sometimes we have too many wild oats as baggage in our souls, when our words are offensive; when our talk becomes too sharp; when our faces have two sides; when our jokes are distasteful;

when we cut each other down; when we talk negative about our pastors and leaders in our churches. Maybe our integrity or lack of it is our wild oats. I am afraid that we Christians are sometimes our own worst enemies. We must repent and let Jesus clean up our hearts so that we plant pure seeds and care for the crops so Jesus will have a bountiful harvest of souls in his kingdom.

2 Chronicles 7:14

If my people, which are called by my name, shall humble themselves and pray, and seek my face and turn from their wicked ways, then I will hear from heaven and will forgive their sins and will heal their land.

James 4:7-8

Submit yourselves, then, to God. Resist the devil, and he will flee from you. Come near to God and He will come near to you. Wash your hands, you sinners, and purify your hearts, you double-minded.

Frank Jones III

Tejin and Rusty,
Getting Cut in Life's Battles

I have had many horses in my life, some not so good, some okay, and a few outstanding. Two of these were Tejin and Rusty, mother and son. When looking back on these outstanding horses, I remembered that they all had one thing in common; they all had been cut and bruised several times.

When Tejin was a colt, she ran through a fence and cut herself on the brisket, which required treatment for two or three weeks. Later when she was about two years old, she cut her foot, right above the hoof, badly on wire. This took me weeks of cleaning and bandaging before it healed properly.

Rusty also had several cuts and scrapes before he learned to respect solid objects, one being a barn that took off a lot of skin on his head.

Working with and administering care to these horses developed a close relationship between them and me. They learned to respect fences, barns, and trailers and trust me when I rode them into unknown situations.

This seems so much like many that I have known, myself included, that many times it is from the many cuts and bruises of life that we pursue God for help. Maybe we learn we can't do it on our own. Maybe it is in our trials that we develop a trust, a relationship, and a dialog with God. But whatever or however we turn to the Lord Jesus and make Him Lord of our lives, we start to realize what He has done for us and begin to trust Him to lead and guide us in our daily lives.

So rejoice in good times and in bad times, it is important in developing you into the person you are meant to be.

Your brother in Christ,

Frankie

Psalms 18:6

In my distress I called upon the Lord, and cried out to my God; He heard my voice from His temple, and my cry came before Him, even to His ears.

1 Peter 1:6,7

In this you greatly rejoice, though now for a little while, if need be, you have been grieved by various trials, that the genuineness of your faith, being much more precious than gold that perishes, though it is tested by fire, may be found to praise, honor, and glory at the revelation of Jesus Christ.

WATCHING PARKER

On July 6, 2002 our daughter, Amy, and son-in-law, Doug, had their first child. Her name is Parker and they are so proud of their precious baby, as we are too. Watching her grow up is so fun to watch. Amy calls almost every day to report what she is doing next. At first all of her needs were met by her mother and father and she just looked around, ate, and slept, but later she began to develop her personality.

She would smile, laugh, cry, play, and start to want things. Some food she wouldn't like and some she would. When she started to crawl and pull up things got exciting. She started trying everything good and bad. Seems like everything had to go into the mouth to get a taste of everything in her world not knowing yet if it was good or bad, but driven to check it out. All this time her mother and father would be watching and caring for her, helping her to make the right choices, and comforting her when she made wrong ones, or fell, or bumped and bruised herself.

All this time mom and dad just wanted her to smile, laugh, be happy, be healthy, and show them love. They would yearn for her to say Mama or Daddy. Even the grandparents wanted to hear her call out Mimi or Papa. That is really all that the parents wanted from her with great expectations that she knew who they were and would call on their name, reach up to crawl in their lap as they reached to pick her up and loved on her.

Doesn't this sound like how we are with God? We run around trying everything in our path that looks interesting, good or bad, just because it is there. We fall, get bruised, hurt, injured, and wonder why these things happen to us when all the time we have a loving God that is there watching and waiting for us to reach up and call on His name, the name of Jesus. He wants to reach down to pick us up and love on us as we sit in His lap. He wants us to be happy, healthy, comforted, safe, wise, and make right choices. He just wants to be acknowledged by us with a smile of love, a praise of who He is and a worship of calling on His name. So listen to His voice and He will guide you and care for you and meet your needs according to His will in your life. Seek Him and you will find Him, call on His name and He will come to you with great love and expectations for you.

Your brother in Christ Jesus,

Frankie

Luke 18:16-17

But Jesus called the children to him and said, "Let the little children come to me, and do not hinder them, for the kingdom of God belongs to such as these. I tell you the truth, anyone who will not receive the kingdom of God like a little child will never enter it."

07/15/03

WHAT'S COOKING IN THE KITCHEN?

Did you ever realize how important the kitchen is in someone's home? Most places I've been, you go into the house through the kitchen instead of the front door. Even when you go through the front door it is usually close to the kitchen. I believe that is because there is always something going on in the kitchen. We may live and relax in the living room but we prepare our food, cook it, and clean up in the kitchen.

There is a lot of stuff in the kitchen, things like bright light, canned food, frozen food, meat, vegetables, stove for cooking, refrigerator for keeping food cold, sinks for cleaning, cabinets and drawers for storing many things, and all sorts of conveniences for making it easier to prepare meals. Boy, what a place! It must be important. It must also be clean so people will want to eat and feed there.

While driving the other day, I was praying and asking God what is it that you want me to do. It jumped into my spirit, just take care of your kitchen and I realized it was my heart. I believe it is from the heart that our actions and our mouth operate. I think when we look at our hearts it is a lot like a kitchen. It is a place where things abide, good and bad. It is a place where the spirit of God dwells. It is a place where we store things, like the word of God, love, happiness, and it can be a place of hate and bitterness which is not good, not clean.

If we keep our hearts full of the love of God, keep our hearts clean, free from things like hate, rage, bitterness, and a judgmental spirit then I believe that people will want to be fed by you however that may be. Let us listen to that still small voice to direct us in our actions and our words and let us give God the glory.   Your brother in Christ,

Frankie

Parables of a Rancher's Life   Frank W. Jones III

Who or What is Controlling Your Life?

What area of our life are we withholding from God today? In what areas do we choose to remain in control? In what part of our life would we prefer that God ignore? In what part of our life would we rather He not snoop?

When we look at these questions the Holy Spirit begins to work on us convicting us of things that need to be broken in our lives to have a closer relationship with our Lord and Savior and our Father in heaven. We can choose to be obedient to God's call in our lives to only the degree that we want to, but that is like reading the bible and tearing out the parts we don't like. We say that doesn't apply to us today, it has lost interpretation over the years or maybe just don't read the bible at all so we don't have to face it.

We live in a world where we are losing our freedoms in every direction we turn, so to give our lives to Jesus fully seems to be out of the question. We think that we will be called to do more than we want to or have to give up something we really like to do. All I can say to that is that I know God wants to bless his people and promises us more abundant life not less. When we allow ourselves to be broken, we don't lose our spirit or personality we only open up ourselves to the will of God and the obedience it takes to follow it. It is like breaking a spirited horse. He will always be quick and spirited, but when broken, he will follow the will of his rider. So it is with God and his children.

Let us not be afraid to be obedient to God's call in our lives, whatever it might be. We do have free will to choose our present and future. Let us remember, "Greater is He that lives in me than he that lives in the world" 1 John 4:4. This world only lasts for a while, but eternity is forever.

Your Brother In Christ Jesus,

Frankie Jones III

Whose Voice Do You Listen To?

One afternoon in the spring of 2003, I decided to plant a food plot for deer. This plot was about 8 acres and I wanted to plant about fifty pounds per acre. I was using a broadcast seeder and then I would disk in the seed and wait for a rain. Setting this seeder to plant the correct amount is difficult, but I had used it many times before so I knew how to set it.

I went to town and stopped by Windmill Feed to pick up 8 or 10 sacks of maize seed. The voice of reason told me that 8 acres needs eight fifty-pound sacks. The more I reasoned and thought I had better get ten sacks just to be sure I had enough. Bill brought the seed around on his forklift and we unloaded it. After putting ten sacks on the truck, that still small voice whispered into my ear, get two more sacks. My voice of reason said back that two extra sacks would be enough, so I only got ten sacks and not twelve.

I went home and started planting the field, being careful to calibrate the seeder as closely as I could, but just as you probably expected by now, I ran out before I finished the field. I needed about two more sacks. I left the best part of the field unplanted to remind me to listen closely when the Holy Spirit speaks to me especially beyond my reasoning.

Maybe we all need to realize that there is reasoning that comes from us and then there is a voice from God that speaks to our spirit within us, but we have to except this voice on faith and believe it.

One thing I have learned is that the voice of the Holy Spirit is never wrong, so let's turn up our receivers and follow the voice of God.

Your brother in Christ Jesus,

Frankie

John 4:10

When he has brought out all his own, he goes on ahead of them, and his sheep follow him because they know his voice.

Hebrews 3:7 & 8

So as the Holy Spirit says: "Today, if you hear his voice, do not harden your hearts as you did in the rebellion, during the time of testing in the desert."

05/01/03

Working Clay with Mama Gladys

My grandmother, Gladys Jones, was an artist and a potter. As children, she would often let us mold things on the potter's wheel. She was always teaching us about the clay and how to work it, mold it, store it, and select it. She would keep several colors of clay in plastic bags thoroughly moistened and out of the sun so that it would not dry out and crack or crumble. Then we would select a clay, add moisture, knead it, and put a portion on the potter's wheel. As the wheel would turn we would take our hands; keeping them wet so that while molding the clay they would become part of the clay; gently shaping the clay to the desired vessel. I wasn't very good, but I wasn't the potter, I was the student or maybe the clay. When finished, my grandmother would always date and initial the vessel then place it into a kiln to expose the vessel to extreme heat and fire to make it strong and useful. These vessels would be used for things like coffee cups, bowls, pitchers, and many other things.

I never realized that my grandmother was teaching me something about how God molds and makes us into a useful vessel for Him. Molding clay is unique soil that holds moisture very well. Without a lot of organic matter mixed in with it, it is not advantageous for any other use. Clay by itself holds water and in our case, it holds living water, the Holy Spirit. So we must let God mold and make us into vessels to hold and distribute living water like a cup. It not only holds but pours out, refreshes and lets others draw from itself. So I believe it is so important to be a vessel filled with the Holy Spirit, the living water to be refreshed and to refresh others. We need to be continually filled and renewed so we won't dry out and crack and crumble.

Your brother in Christ,

Frankie

Isaiah 64:8
But now, O Lord, You are our Father; we are the clay, and you our potter; and all we are the work of Your hand.

Jeremiah 18:4
And the vessel that he made of clay was marred in the hand of the potter; so he made it again into another vessel, as it seemed good to the potter to make.

Roman 9:21
Does not the potter have power over the clay, from the same lump to make one vessel for honor and another for dishonor?

06/04/02

THE END

Author Frank W. Jones lll
Angel Canyon Publishing House
PO Box 924, Utopia, TX 78884
Author Page:
http://www.angelcanyonpublishing.com/author-frank-w-jones/

CONTACT ME

2993 W. Sabinal Rd.
PO Box 91, Utopia, TX 78884
fwj3.bcranch@gmail.com

Find me on facebook

https://www.facebook.com/frankie.jones.161?fref=ts

Parables of a Rancher's Life   Frank W. Jones III

Parables of a Rancher's Life   Frank W. Jones III

Made in the USA
San Bernardino, CA
05 April 2014